# DECISION MAKING & PROBLEM SOLVING

# CREATING SUCCESS

## The best-selling series is back and better than ever

## MARCH 2013

**Because you only have one chance in life to make a good impression.**

# DECISION MAKING & PROBLEM SOLVING

## JOHN ADAIR

## CREATING SUCCESS

Previously published by the Institute of Personnel and Development as *Decision Making and Problem Solving* 1997 and 1999
First published in 2007 by Kogan Page Limited as *Decision Making and Problem Solving Strategies*
Reissued 2010
Reissued in 2013 as *Decision Making and Problem Solving*
Reprinted 2013

| | | |
|---|---|---|
| 2nd Floor, 45 Gee Street | 1518 Walnut Street, Suite 1100 | 4737/23 Ansari Road |
| London EC1V 3RS | Philadelphia PA 19102 | Daryaganj |
| United Kingdom | USA | New Delhi 110002 |
| www.koganpage.com | | India |

© John Adair, 1997, 1999, 2007, 2010, 2013

The right of John Adair to be identified as the author of this work has been asserted by him in accordance with the Copyright, Designs and Patents Act 1988.

ISBN      978 0 7494 6696 1
E-ISBN   978 0 7494 6697 8

British Library Cataloguing-in-Publication Data

A CIP record for this book is available from the British Library.

Library of Congress Cataloging-in-Publication Data

Adair, John Eric, 1934-
  Decision making and problem solving / John Adair. – 2nd Edition.
    pages cm
  Includes index.
    ISBN 978-0-7494-6696-1 – ISBN (invalid) 978-0-7494-6697-8 (ebk.)   1. Decision making.   2. Problem solving.   3. Thought and thinking.   I. Title.
    HD30.23.A3 2013
    658.4'03–dc23
                                                                                          2012045519

Typeset by Graphicraft Limited, Hong Kong
Printed and bound by CPI Group (UK) Ltd, Croydon, CR0 4YY

# CONTENTS

# Key problem-solving strategies   43

# How to generate ideas   53

# Thinking outside the box   61

## Developing your thinking skills  73

## ABOUT THE AUTHOR

John Adair is now widely regarded as the world's leading authority on leadership and leadership development. The author of 30 books on the subject, he has been named as one of the 40 people worldwide who have contributed most to the development of management thought and practice.

Educated at St Paul's School, John Adair has enjoyed a varied and colourful career. He served as adjutant in a Bedouin regiment in the Arab Legion, worked as a deckhand on an Arctic trawler and had a spell as an orderly in a hospital operating theatre. After attending Cambridge University he became Senior Lecturer in Military History and Leadership Training Adviser at the Royal Military Academy, Sandhurst, before becoming the first Director of Studies at St George's House in Windsor Castle and then Associate Director of the Industrial Society. Later he became the world's first Professor in Leadership Studies at the University of Surrey. He also helped to found Europe's first Centre for Leadership Studies at the University of Exeter.

John Adair now acts as a national and international adviser on leadership development. His recent books, published by Kogan Page, include *Not Bosses But Leaders*, *The Inspirational Leader*, *How to Grow Leaders* and *Leadership and Motivation*.

# INTRODUCTION

There are three forms of applied thinking that we all need: decision making, problem solving and creative thinking. These overlap considerably but they can be distinguished.

Decision making is about deciding what action to take; it usually involves choice between options. The object of problem solving is usually a solution, answer or conclusion. The outcome of creative thinking, by contrast, is new ideas.

Any leader such as yourself who aspires to excellence obviously has a vested interest in seeing that the best decisions are taken, that problems are solved in the optimum way and that the creative ideas and innovations so necessary for tomorrow's business flow freely. Of course, everyone in the team or organization should be engaged in meeting these essential requirements. But you are the one who is called to provide the intellectual leadership that is needed. Are you willing to do so?

One step towards that end that you should definitely take is to become master of the *processes of practical thinking*, the processes that lie behind all effective decision making, problem solving and creative thinking. You cannot guarantee *outcomes* – for luck or chance plays a part in all human affairs – but you can at least make sure that you use the well tried-and-tested processes of thinking to some purpose. You own that responsibility. For my part, the aim of this book is to equip you with the necessary knowledge of those processes and to help you to acquire skill in using them.

One further word. Forget the idea that *thinking* is somehow a painful and laborious feeling in the mind, a kind of headache that is best avoided if possible. Thinking is fun. By fun here I do not really mean a diversion that affords enjoyment. For the word also means an activity that engages one's interest or imagination, an activity that may prove to be more than a diversion and may involve challenge and hard work but is still a source of enjoyment. If you come to love thinking for yourself you will learn naturally to do it well.

As Roy Thompson, one of the greatest businessmen of our time, once said, 'If I have any advice to pass on, as a successful man, it is this: if one wants to be successful, one must think; one must think until it hurts.' He added that, 'From my close observation, I can say that there are few people indeed who are prepared to perform this arduous and tiring work.' Are you one of them?

In the following pages we shall explore some practical ways in which you can improve your skills in this key area. By the time you have worked through the book you should:

- understand the way in which the mind works and the principles of effective thinking;

- have a clear framework for decision making;

- be aware of the relation between decision making and problem solving;

- be able to use a unified model for both making decisions and solving problems;

- have sharpened up your creative thinking skills;

- be in a position to chart a way forwards for improving your thinking skills across the board.

# YOUR MIND AT WORK

Behind your practical, everyday thinking there lies the most complex thing in the known universe: the human mind. Nobody hires and pays you nowadays for your physical strength. You are employed because you have a mind – and can use it effectively.

There is a vital distinction between brain and mind. Take a computer as an analogy. Your brain is what you see if you open up the back of the computer – all those chips and circuits – whereas the mind is what appears dynamically on the screen. In this book we are focusing on the mind, for that is accessible to us without peering into the skull.

There are two aspects to the mind: the information it can store in the memory, and what it can do. What we call technical or professional knowledge usually involves both. You not only need knowledge about a subject but you also need to be able to apply it in a variety of unforeseen situations.

Such applications of professional knowledge invariably involve the activities of decision making and problem solving. A doctor, for example, is problem solving when he or she tries to diagnose the cause of your weak left leg. Indeed, decision making and problem solving are so bound up with particular kinds of information or knowledge – areas of professional competence – that we find it hard to think of them in the abstract.

Are there any generic or transferable skills in these areas? Yes, I believe there are. The characteristic function of the mind is to think. So let's leave on one side for a moment the memory or database function of the mind and concentrate on its primary role as a thinking tool. What is the nature of thinking? Are there any universal principles? If so, how can you use these principles to sharpen your skills as a practical thinker?

## IS YOUR BRAIN WORKING NOW?

The physical base of your mind is of course your brain, the grey matter housed in your head. Your brain is composed of about 10,000 million cells. In fact it has more cells than there are people on the face of the earth! Each one of those cells can link up with approximately 10,000 of its neighbours, which gives you some 1 plus 800 noughts of possible combinations.

Our *potential* brain power is known to be far greater than the actual power it achieves. No one has remotely approached the limits of it. One estimate suggests that we use no more than about 10 per cent of our brain power. So don't be worried by the fact that you are losing about 400 brain cells every day – indeed, if you do not exercise your mind throughout your life your brain will shrink at a faster rate. *Use it or lose it!*

Before we go any further, I suggest we double-check that all your 10,000 million brain cells are warmed up and working properly by trying to solve some problems. Actually, the three problems below require only about 3,000 million brain cells, so they will not take long or cause us much delay!

Two other points before we begin. The three problems are not just brain-teasers: they illustrate principles about thinking.

So I am not playing games with you. Second, I am not going to give you the answers in this chapter to the first two problems, though I shall do so later. This can be a bit frustrating. But I have a reason for leaving you in suspense. For reasons I shall explain later, I believe that the answers to problems 1 and 2 – assuming that you cannot solve them immediately – may come to you later.

## Problem 1    The nine dots

Take a piece of paper larger than this page and put on it a pattern of nine dots, like this:

● ● ●

● ● ●

● ● ●

Now connect up the dots by four straight consecutive lines (that is, without taking your pen or pencil off the paper). You should be able to complete this task within three minutes.

## Problem 2    The six matchsticks

Place six matchsticks – preferably of the wooden variety – on a flat surface. Now arrange the matchsticks in a pattern of four equilateral (ie equal-sided) triangles. You may not break the matchsticks – that is the only rule. Again, you should be able to do it within three minutes. There are at least two solutions, but I want the best one.

## Problem 3    Who owns the zebra?

Having got the two easy ones safely behind you – well done if you have solved both those problems – we come now to something a little more demanding, so you must call up your reserve brain cells.

The world record for solving *both* parts of this problem is 10 minutes. So I will give you 30 minutes which, I am sure you will agree, is overgenerous of me!

1 There are five houses, each with a front door of a different colour, and inhabited by people of different nationalities, with different pets and drinks. Each person eats a different kind of food.

2 The Australian lives in the house with the red door.

3 The Italian owns the dog.

4 Coffee is drunk in the house with the green door.

5 The Ukrainian drinks tea.

6 The house with the green door is immediately to the right (your right) of the house with the ivory door.

7 The mushroom-eater owns snails.

8 Apples are eaten in the house with the yellow door.

9 Milk is drunk in the middle house.

10 The Norwegian lives in the first house on the left.

11 The person who eats onions lives in the house next to the person with the fox.

12 Apples are eaten in the house next to the house where the horse is kept.

13 The cake-eater drinks orange juice.

14 The Japanese eats bananas.

15 The Norwegian lives next to the house with the blue door.

Now, who drinks water and who owns the zebra?

# THE FUNCTIONS OF THE MIND

Let's now look at how the mind works. I suggest that there are three main functions: analysing, synthesizing and imagining, and valuing.

In the applied forms of effective thinking – decision making, problem solving, and creative or innovative thinking – all three of these functions are at work. It is their underlying health that largely determines the quality of your thought. Few people have them in harmonious balance, as shown in Figure 1.1. Most of us are better at one rather than the other two.

Our differing mental strengths are a powerful reason why we need each other: effective thinking in all its forms is both a solitary and a social activity. You should always see yourself alternately as thinking alone (for yourself) and as thinking with others – either face to face or, as in this case, by reading or some other method of communication. Still, it is a good idea to seek to develop your skills in the weaker areas, like a person building up muscles in a limb through exercise: you will not always have

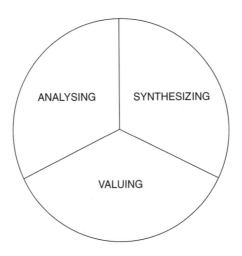

**Figure 1.1**   The main functions of the mind

the right people at hand to correct your bias towards a particular function.

## Analysing

The word 'analyse' comes from a Greek verb meaning 'to loosen', and it means separating a whole into its constituent parts. In tackling the 'Who owns the zebra?' exercise you were using your analytical skills of dissection, trying to break down the task into its parts.

Analytical thinking is closely related to logical or step-by-step reasoning. You may have noticed that one of the skills you were using in tackling that particular problem was your power of deduction.

Logic has two main parts: *deduction and induction*. Deduction means literally to subtract or take away. It is the process of deducing a conclusion from what is known or assumed. More specifically, it is a question of inferring from the general to the particular. 'All swans are birds. This is a swan. Therefore...' Induction works the other way round. It is the process of inferring or verifying a general law or principle from the observation of particular instances – the core of the 'scientific method'.

## EXERCISE 1  SPOT THE FALLACY

Can you spot the logical fallacy in the following statement?

The chief executive of St Samaritan's Hospital Trust cleared his throat and began.

'Thank you all for coming to this meeting, which is, as you know, about how to improve the quality of our service in this hospital. To begin with I have decided to sack all the surgeons and physicians over the age of 55 years. Look at these letters! I have had five letters of complaint about the abruptness and lack of communication of doctors here, and two mentioned that the doctors are too old or have passed their "sell-by" date. The way to deal with this problem is to lower the average age of the staff, so I am going to ask everyone to take voluntary retirement at 55. Any questions before we move on to the next item on the agenda – litter in the corridors?'

For the main part, unlike the manager in the 'Spot the fallacy' exercise (above), most of us are quite good at analysing problems or situations. This is not surprising, as much of our education is concerned with developing our deductive/inductive powers (mathematics, sciences, history, and literature) and sharpening our analytical skills.

You may now like to look at the solution to the 'Who owns the zebra?' problem (see page 83). As you will see, it combines a test of your powers of reasoning or logical thinking with the important principle of trial and error. When you are faced with two alternatives – such as two roads at a junction without signposts that lead in the right general direction – there is no other way but to try each one in turn. In the case of this exercise, using a computer would save you time. But in real life you may, as they say, have to 'suck it and see'. Decision making is not an exact science.

## Synthesizing

It is not easy to give a single label to the second function. Synthesizing – another Greek word – is putting or placing things together to make a whole. It is the reverse process of analysing. You can synthesize things with your hands, which you do whenever you assemble or make anything. All products and services are the results of syntheses. But you can also do it mentally.

When that happens, another faculty is called into play – imagination. Now, imagination works in pictures, and a picture is a whole that is more than the sum of its parts. If you shut your eyes for a moment and think of your house or your car, you see a picture. In fact, it is almost impossible not to see a picture. Your computer-like memory flashes it up on the inner screen of your mind very quickly. What you see is neither a pile of bricks, in the case of your house, nor a heap of car components, but in each case a whole.

If, so to speak, you turn up the volume knob of your imagination, you can see things that do not exist. Imagine, for example, a 56-metre-tall man... This road takes us into how to generate ideas, the subject to be explored more fully in Chapter 5.

The link between creativity and the synthesizing process is clear when you contemplate how nature works. A baby arrives whole and it grows. Nature is *holistic*. A famous South African, Field Marshal Jan Smuts, who was also a keen agricultural scientist, coined the word holism to describe nature's way of creating wholes by ordering or grouping various units together. The essential realities in nature, Smuts argued, are these irreducible wholes. If analysed into parts, they lose their essential holistic quality. As the poet William Wordsworth put it, 'We murder to dissect.' Your mind has a holistic dimension. It can think holistically – in terms of wholes – as well as analytically (taking wholes to bits).

## Valuing

The third function comes into play in such mental activities as establishing success criteria, evaluating, appraising performance, and judging people – as, for example, in a selection interview. *Criticism* (from the Greek word for a judge) is a form of valuing.

Incidentally, criticism, as commonly understood, most often suggests disapproval – some sort of a negative judgement. But in its more formal use it can suggest neutral analysis or even approving evaluation. Judgement is not always unfavourable.

In all valuing there is an objective (outside yourself) element and a subjective one. We are all born with the capacity to value. What we *actually* value – our values – depends very largely upon our environment and its culture.

Values are rather like colours. What is the colour of grass? 'Easy', you reply. 'It is green.' But scientists tell us that grass has no intrinsic colour: it is merely reflecting light in the wave band that we call green. The structure of our eyes is also a factor. Our subjective contribution to the perception of colour is significant. Being colour-blind to certain shades of the red–green spectrum – fortunately not to the greenest of grass – I am personally very aware of that fact.

The word *value* comes from a market metaphor: it is what you have to give in order to receive something across the counter. The invention of money revolutionized bartering. One merit of money is that it was a universal measuring stick. But there are plenty of other values that enter into any form of decision making, especially in business today. (See Exercise 2.)

## EXERCISE 2  VALUES AT WORK

Make a list of all the values – apart from financial value (profit) – which might influence any business decision over the coming 10 years.

Check to see whether the organization you work for has issued a statement of its corporate values. If so, obtain a copy and underline what you judge to be the master value in it.

How far do your organization's values overlap with your own philosophy of life?

Whether or not values in the popular sense have a separate existence, and where they come from if not from ourselves, are philosophical questions that lie beyond the scope of this book. But in all thinking there is a strong case for acting as if truth – one member of the trinity of goodness, truth, and beauty – really does exist 'out there'. It would be impossible, for example, to explain the immense success story of modern science without the working belief of scientists such as Einstein that the truth is 'out there' waiting to be discovered.

## INTRODUCING THE DEPTH MIND PRINCIPLE

As we all know, we have subconscious and unconscious minds. But we are not so aware of the vital part that the dimension that I have named the Depth Mind plays in our thinking. You can, as it were, analyse, synthesize and value in your sleep or when you are consciously doing something quite different, like gardening or washing the dishes. Far from being chaotic, the Depth Mind plays a large part in scientific discovery and creative art. It is also the source of intuition – that all-important sixth sense.

Conrad Hilton was trying to buy an old Chicago hotel. A few days before the deadline for sealed bids, Hilton submitted a bid for US $165,000, a figure he had reached by some hasty calculations, as he was busy on other things at the time. He went to bed that night feeling vaguely disturbed and awoke the following morning with the feeling that his bid was not high enough. Another figure kept coming to him out of his Depth Mind – US $180,000. 'It satisfied me. It seemed fair. It felt right. I changed my bid to the higher figure on that hunch. When the envelopes were opened the closest bid to mine was US $179,000.'

Can you think of a similar decision or problem in your experience when your Depth Mind has played a similar role?

## CHECKLIST: LISTENING TO YOUR DEPTH MIND

|                                                                                                                          | Yes | No |
|--------------------------------------------------------------------------------------------------------------------------|-----|----|
| Do you have a friendly and positive attitude to your Depth Mind? Do you *expect* it to work for you?                      | ☐   | ☐  |
| Where possible, do you build into your plans time to 'sleep on it', so as to give your Depth Mind an opportunity to contribute? | ☐   | ☐  |
| Do you deliberately seek to employ your Depth Mind to help you to:                                                        | ☐   | ☐  |
|    analyse a complex situation                                                                             | ☐   | ☐  |
|    restructure a problem                                                                                   | ☐   | ☐  |
|    reach value judgements?                                                                                 | ☐   | ☐  |
| Have you experienced waking up next morning to find that your unconscious mind has resolved some problem or made some decision for you? | ☐   | ☐  |
| Do you see your Depth Mind as being like a computer? Remember the computer proverb: Garbage in, garbage out.             | ☐   | ☐  |
| Do you keep a notebook or pocket tape-recorder at hand to capture fleeting or half-formed ideas?                          | ☐   | ☐  |
| Do you think you can benefit from understanding how the Depth Minds of other people work?                                | ☐   | ☐  |

Roy Thompson, in his autobiography *After I Was Sixty* (1975), explains how the Depth Mind works.

*When a new problem arose, I would think it over and, if the answer was not immediately apparent, I would let it go for a while, and it was as if it went the rounds of the brain cells looking for guidance that could be retrieved, for by the next morning, when I examined the problem again, more often than not the solution came up right away. That judgement seems to have come to me almost unconsciously, and my conviction is that during the time I was not consciously considering the problem, my subconscious had been turning it over and relating it to my memory.*

The use of your Depth Mind in decision making, problem solving and creative thinking is such an important principle that I shall return to it later. The million-dollar question is: Can we develop our Depth Mind capability? My answer is: Yes, we can. And the first step is *awareness* that it both exists and works. The secret of effective thinking is working with the natural grain of your mind – *go with the flow* as they say, but see if you can steer the boat.

# KEY POINTS

- We are called *homo sapiens* on account of our minds. The human capacity to exercise the mind – the activity we call thinking – is truly remarkable. Yet few of us use our minds to anything near their full capacity.

- Thinking is to regard or examine in the mind, to reflect or to ponder. As we experience it, thinking is a single stream of consciousness. But we can discern three interweaving currents in thinking to some purpose: analysing, synthesizing and valuing.

- *Analysing*, the first function, tends to be highly developed by Western education. It is the mental ability to take things – material and non-material – to bits, to separate them into their component parts. It is related, but not identical, to logical or step-by-step thinking.

- *Synthesizing* is the reverse process of putting things together to form a whole. When the resultant whole is formed from parts previously thought to be unconnected, when it looks new and has real value, then synthesizing has become *creative*.

- *Valuing*, the third main function in purposive thinking, is self-explanatory. Even in the strictest schools of science or logic, it is impossible to exclude value. We are all valuing creatures; our actual values are largely shaped by our cultural experience. Of course, by helping us to escape out of the cultural box of our particular lives we encounter more universal values: goodness, truth and beauty.

- These functions – analysing, synthesizing and valuing – can do their work at the unconscious level I have called the Depth Mind. Indeed, where complex decisions have to be made, problems solved or truly creative products involved, the Depth Mind is a vital dimension in the effective use of your mind.

We do not think as long as things run along smoothly for us. It is only when the routine is disrupted by the intrusion of a difficulty, obstacle or challenge that we are forced to stop drifting and to think what we are going to do.

JOHN DEWEY

# THE ART OF EFFECTIVE DECISION MAKING

> There is a time when we must firmly choose
> the course we will follow, or the relentless drift
> of events will make the decision.
> FRANKLIN D ROOSEVELT

In decision making there is a classic five-step approach that you should find extremely helpful. That does not mean you should follow it blindly in all situations. It is a fairly natural sequence of thought, however, and so even without the formal framework you would tend to follow this mental path. The advantage of making it conscious is that it is easier to be swiftly aware when a step is missing or – more probably – has been performed without understanding or intention.

It is useful to think of the five steps on page 19 as five notes of music. Logically they should be played in strict sequence. But the mind darts about. The notes can be combined in different sequences and mental chords. Thinking is not a tidy process, but it should be done with a sense of order.

Remember that we are not talking here about just big decisions, for there's a lot more to running a business than making one life-or-death decision. Indeed no decision, no matter how big, is any more than a small fraction of the total outcome. Yes, some decisions are much bigger than others, and some are forks in the road. But it is really more the case that a much larger number of small decisions have a cumulative result. By hindsight we can usually identify those few pivotal decisions, but it is really the stream of smaller decisions over time, made and executed with a craftsman's skill, that yields great outcomes.

## DEFINE THE OBJECTIVE

Do you know what you are trying to achieve? You do need to be clear – or as clear as possible – about where you want to get to. Otherwise the whole process of decision making is obscured in a cloud. As the proverb says, *If you do not know what port you are heading for, any wind is the right wind.*

If you are in doubt about your aim, try writing it down. Leave it for a day or two, if time allows, and then look at it again. You may be able to see at once how it can be sharpened or focused.

## COLLECT RELEVANT INFORMATION

The next skill is concerned with collecting and sifting relevant information. Some of it will be immediately apparent, but other data may be missing. It is a good principle not to make decisions in the absence of critically important information that is not immediately to hand, provided that a planned delay is acceptable.

Remember the distinction between *available* and *relevant* information. One classic mistake is to look at the broad decision

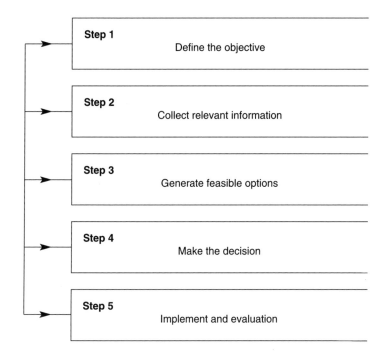

**Step 1**
Define the objective

**Step 2**
Collect relevant information

**Step 3**
Generate feasible options

**Step 4**
Make the decision

**Step 5**
Implement and evaluation

**Figure 2.1** The classic approach to decision making

and then turn to the information we have that will help us decide. Some thinkers do not, however, look at the information at their disposal and ask themselves, 'Is this relevant?' Instead they wonder, 'How can I use it?' They are confusing two kinds of information – as is illustrated on page 20.

Life would be much simpler if you could just use the information at your disposal, rather than that which you really need to make the decision! So often quantities of data are advanced – there are acres of it on the internet – that merely add bulk to, say, a management report without giving its recommendations any additional (metaphorical) weight.

The rapid growth of methods of communication such as faxes, voice mail, e-mail, junk mail and the internet has now contributed to a new disease: Information Overload Syndrome. A recent international survey of 1,300 managers listed the new disease's

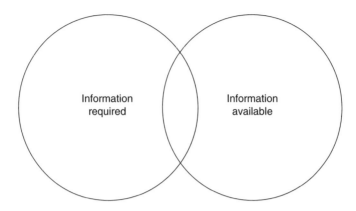

Information
required

Information
available

**Figure 2.2** Information categories

symptoms, which included a feeling of inability to cope with the incoming data as it piles up, resulting sometimes in mental stress and even physical illness requiring time off work. The survey found that such overload is a growing problem among managers – almost all of whom expect it to become worse. Executives and their juniors say they are caught in a dilemma: everyone tells them that they should have more information so they can make better decisions, but the proliferation of sources makes it impossible to keep abreast of the data.

The growth of information has been relentless. The *New York Times* contains as much distinct information every day as the average seventeenth-century person encountered in a lifetime. No wonder that half the managers surveyed complained of information overload, partly caused by enormous amounts of unsolicited information. The same proportion also expected the incredible expansion of the internet to intensify the problem year-on-year. To avoid succumbing to Information Overload Syndrome you need all the skills described in this book!

Suppose that the overlap between information *required* and information *available* is not sufficient: what do you do? Obviously you set about obtaining more of the information *required* category. But getting information or – to use a grander description – doing research incurs costs in time and money. Your organization may not be in the business of making profits, but it certainly has to be businesslike when it comes to containing costs.

What the graph below suggests is that you usually acquire a great deal of relevant information in a relatively short time and, possibly, at a relatively low cost in money. But the line soon curves towards a plateau. You will find yourself spending more and more time to discover less and less relevant information. For example, if you and I sat next to each other at a dinner, I should learn all the really important things about you in the first half hour. The longer we talked, the smaller the increments of knowledge about you would become. After three hours I should be down to discussing relatively fine details.

## GENERATE FEASIBLE OPTIONS

Notice the word *options* rather than *alternatives*. An alternative is literally one of two courses open. Decision makers who lack skill tend to jump far too quickly to the either–or alternatives. They do

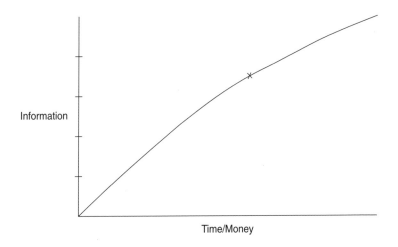

**Figure 2.3** The time/information curve

not give enough time and mental energy to generating at least three or four possibilities. As Bismarck used to say to his generals, 'You can be sure that if the enemy has only two courses of action open to him, he will choose the third.' Alfred Sloan, the renowned President of General Motors, was even known to adjourn meetings in which he was presented with two alternatives. 'Please go away and generate more options,' he would say.

You need to open your mind into wide focus to consider all possibilities, and that is where generating ideas (see Chapter 5) comes in. But then your valuing faculty must come into play in order to identify the *feasible* options. 'Feasible' means capable of being done or carried out or realized. If it is feasible it has some real likelihood of being workable. It can attain the end you have in mind.

In moving along the lobster pot (see Figure 2.4) from the feasible options (no more than five or six, for the mind finds it difficult to handle more) to three options and then to two (the true alternatives), the principle to bear in mind is that *it is easier to falsify something than to verify it.*

Suppose you are choosing between five medium-sized estate cars for your family. It is easy to eliminate the unsuitable ones.

As you work on it, for example, you may discover that one of the cars is 9 inches longer than the others, which will cause you a problem given the size of your garage. As for a second car, on studying the specifications you cannot see why it is £1,200 more expensive than the rest – apart from its prestigious name. So you drop that one too, leaving you now with three choices. You will notice another principle coming into play here, which (subject to the information/time curve) does take most of the pain out of decision making. Let me continue with the car example. Because your partner does not like the colours of the Toyota model and, being an artist by profession, feels strongly about it, you are able to eliminate that one. Your alternatives are now the Nissan and the Peugeot.

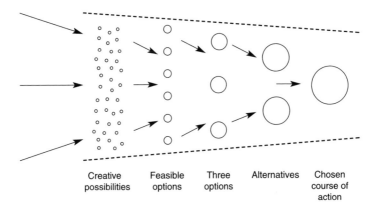

| Creative possibilities | Feasible options | Three options | Alternatives | Chosen course of action |

**Figure 2.4** The lobster pot model

You have just read this book and so, being persuaded by its argument, you decide to trade some more time for some more information, and test drive the alternative cars. Both feel great and perform really well. You know that either will serve your purpose. It is now a question of money and the availability of the colours your partner likes. One of the dealers offers you a much better price and can deliver the right model in the range. Why hesitate?

# MAKE THE DECISION

The critical preliminary activity here is to establish the selection criteria. It is worth dividing them into different levels of priority. (See Figure 2.5)

Unless an option meets the MUST requirements you should discard it. But after the essentials have been satisfied, the list of desirables – highly desirable SHOULDs or pleasant addition MIGHTs – comes into play.

Choosing a car is a relatively simple case, because there is a finite number of models to choose from and a relatively simple list

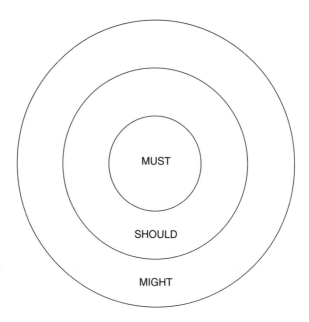

**Figure 2.5** Decision-making criteria

of criteria. In order to help you choose in more complex cases, remember that you can make a decision by:

- listing the advantages and disadvantages;

- examining the consequences of each course;

- testing the proposed course against the yardstick of your aim or objective;

- weighing the risks against the expected gains.

## Assessing risk

What makes decisions really difficult is the factor of high risk. You may recall the conflicting advice of the two proverbs *Look before you leap* and *He who hesitates is lost*. There is an important skill in calculating risk. Calculation sounds mathematical, and there are plenty of management books with 'decision making' in the title that offer various 'probability theories' and statistical methods to take the pain out of risk assessment. Sometimes it can help to assign numbers and calculate in that way, but the contribution of mathematics to this field is very limited. Experience plays a much larger part.

One helpful idea is to define the worst downside – what happens in the worst scenario? Can you accept that, or will it sink you? But in high-risk/high-reward situations, although you may know that you will be sunk if it does not all work out, you may still decide to take the high-risk course because the reward is just too important for you to forgo it.

You then have to address your mind to doing all you can to reduce the risk. It is here that experience, practice, consultation with specialists, reconnaissance and mental rehearsals may all be relevant techniques. You are trying to turn the *possibility* of success into the *probability* of success, but you will not be able to eliminate risk altogether: in this situation there are too many contingencies.

## Assessing consequences

Risk is one aspect of thinking through the consequences of the feasible courses of action.

Consequences come in two forms: manifest and latent. Manifest consequences are ones that, in principle, you can foresee when you make your decision. I say 'in principle' because that does not mean to say that you *did* foresee them. What I mean is that any reasonable person with the knowledge, experience, or skill expected of someone in your position would foresee those consequences. If you try to rob a bank, for example, the *manifest* consequences are obvious to any reasonable person:

- You might become amazingly rich.

- People, including you, might get hurt.

- You could be sent to prison.

*Latent* consequences are different in that they are not nearly so probable, or even possible, and a reasonable person might be forgiven for not seeing the knock-on effects that result from the complex chain of events triggered off by a decision. Admittedly, with the aid of computers it becomes a little easier in certain fields to identify latent consequences, but it is seldom possible to insulate yourself against pleasant or unpleasant surprises. We just cannot foresee the future in that way.

The emergence of *latent* consequences, of course, triggers off another round of decision-making and problem-solving activity. Yet solutions are the seeds of new problems.

Introducing performance-related pay for individuals, for example, solves some motivational problems, but what other problems does it tend to create for teams and organizations, not to mention the individuals concerned?

Fill the quarters of the window in Figure 2.6 with the consequences of a decision to make pay totally performance-related. Review the completed window – remember, you are looking for insights.

I suppose that if we knew all the *latent* consequences of all our decisions at the time of making them, we should soon decide to stay in bed all day and never make another decision! But that decision in itself would have manifest and latent consequences... All that we can do, as humans and not angels or gods, is to make the best decisions we can, given the information and circumstances, and then make other decisions to deal with the latent consequences as they arise.

Remember that there is a big difference between a *wrong* decision and a bad decision. A wrong decision is choosing to dig your only oil well in this place rather than that one. It's an expensive mistake, but the fault lies with the method. A bad decision is launching the space shuttle *Challenger* on a severely cold morning when the contracting engineers responsible for the seals in the engines have predicted a nearly 100 per cent chance that the seals will fail in such conditions. They did – with a tragic loss of life.

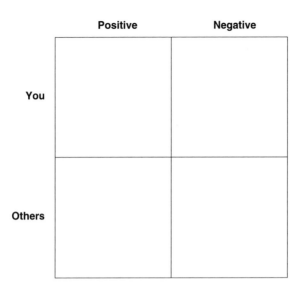

|  | Positive | Negative |
|---|---|---|
| **You** | | |
| **Others** | | |

**Figure 2.6** The outcomes window

Here the method or process of decision making was deliberately ignored or irresponsibly put on one side.

The distinction is important because it separates *outcomes*, which you cannot fully control because of the part that luck or chance plays, from *process*, which you can. Wrong decisions are an inevitable aspect of life, both in our personal and professional lives. We redeem them by learning the lessons they teach us, paying the fees that life charges as cheerfully as we can. But bad decisions are predictable pitfalls; they are unforced errors. They are eminently avoidable if you use the proven processes, methods and techniques outlined in this book.

## IMPLEMENT AND EVALUATE

Decision comes from a Latin verb meaning 'to cut off'. It is related to such cutting words as 'scissors' and 'incision'.

Thinking       Action

**Point of no return**

**Figure 2.7**    The point of no return

What is 'cut off' when you make a decision is the preliminary activity of thinking, especially the business of weighing up the pros and cons of the various courses of action. You now move into the action phase. Out with your cheque book – start talking about delivery dates! Things begin to happen.

It is always worth identifying what I have called the Point of No Return (PNR), a term that comes from aviation. At the half-way point in crossing the Atlantic, it is easier for the pilot to continue to Paris in the event of engine trouble than to turn back to New York. The pilot has passed the PNR and he or she is committed.

In its wider sense the PNR is the point at which it costs you more in various coinages to turn back or change your mind than to continue with a decision that you now know to be an imperfect one. In most decisions you do have a little leeway before you are finally committed: you can still change your mind. Often, as in the case study of Conrad Hilton (see page 12), it is your Depth Mind that double-checks your decision. It either whispers, 'Yes, I am satisfied' or begins an insidious and insistent campaign to make you at least review your decision, if not change your mind.

There is another reason for seeing implementation as a part in the decision-making process rather than the end of it. Your valuing faculty is bound to come into play at some stage in order to evaluate the decision. Did you get it right? Could you have made the decision more quickly or more gracefully, perhaps at less cost to others? All this data goes into your memory bank and informs the Depth Mind, so that the next time you make a similar decision this information about your past may be available to you in the form of a more educated intuition. This is what constitutes what we call experience.

*Remember, your Depth Mind really does work!*

In 2006 some researchers at the University of Amsterdam decided to put the Depth Mind theory to the test. The psychologists asked a group of volunteers to pretend they were about to buy one of four cars. The volunteers were given lots of information about the cars, and one model was much better than the others.

Half the volunteers were given time to ponder the merits of each car, while the others were given puzzles to solve to keep their minds busy. Both groups were then asked to pick the car they would buy.

The results showed that those who restricted themselves to conscious thought were less likely to have chosen the best deal.

Those whose surface minds were occupied with the irrelevant puzzles made better choices. In a second experiment, the volunteers were faced with furniture choices at Ikea.

What the experiments show is that your Depth Mind can deal with more facts and figures than your conscious mind. The latter is good at simple choices, such as buying different towels or different sets of oven mitts. But choices made in complex matters, such as between different houses or cars, are better if your Depth Mind is involved.

The principle, I may add, *always* applies over people decisions, especially the choice of one's life partner. 'I have no other but a woman's reason. I think him so because I think him so,' says one of Shakespeare's heroines. In less eloquent language we might say that it is our Depth Mind that can best process all the complex information that comes from another person and transform it into a simple but profound judgement. Who knows how this work is accomplished in the inner hive of the mind?

> **Take care that the honey does not remain in you in the same state as when you gathered it: bees would have no credit unless they transformed it into something different and better.**
> PETRARCH

# KEY POINTS

- Sometimes it is useful for the mind to have a framework for approaching potentially difficult tasks. In decision making there is such a simple framework of five steps or phases. Think of it more as a spiralling process, like this:

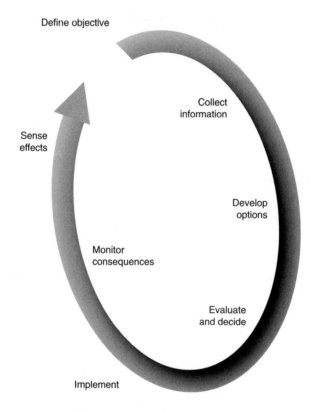

- *Defining the objective* is invariably important in decision making. One useful tip is to write it down, for seeing it in writing often helps you to attain the necessary clarity of mind.

- *Collecting relevant information* involves both surveying the available information and then taking steps to acquire the missing but *relevant* information to the matter in hand.

- *For generating feasible options*, remember the lobster pot model! You should be able to move systematically from a host of possibilities – some of them may be the results of imaginative thinking – to a diminishing set of *feasible* options, the courses of action that are actually practicable given the resources available.

- In *making the decision your chosen success criteria* (the product of the *valuing* function of the mind) come into play. It is useful to grade these yardsticks into the criteria that the proposed course of action MUST, SHOULD and MIGHT meet. You will also need to assess the *risks* involved: what are the *manifest* and the possible *latent* consequences of the decision inview?

- *Implementing and evaluating* the decision should be seen as part of the overall process. You may hardly notice the actual point of decision, just as passengers on a ship may be asleep when their ship crosses the equator line. The 'cut off' point, be it conscious or unconscious, is when thinking ends – your mind is made up – and you move into the action or implementation phase. But you are still evaluating the decision, and up to the Point of No Return (PNR), you can always turn back if the early signs dictate.

- If you have all the required information, the mind goes through the point of decision effortlessly – indeed, do you really have to take a decision? Thus it has been said that 'a decision is the action an executive must take when he or she has information so incomplete that the answer does not suggest itself'.

  **Not to decide is to decide.**
  ENGLISH PROVERB

# SHARING DECISIONS WITH OTHERS

A key issue in leadership is how far the designated leader (appointed or elected) should share decisions with others – team members or colleagues. Of course it is also an issue for all of us – how far should we make our decisions after solitary and silent thought, or how far should we consult others?

## YOUR ROLE AS LEADER

Before looking together at the decision-making aspect of leadership let me put it in context by reminding you of the generic role of *leader* – true for all fields of work and all levels of leadership.

If you look closely at matters involving leadership, there are always three elements or variables:

- the leader – qualities of personality and character;

- the situation – partly constant, partly varying;

- the group – the followers: their needs and values.

In fact, work groups are always different, just as individuals are. After coming together they soon develop a *group personality*. So that which works in one group may not work in another. All groups and organizations are unique.

But that is only half the truth. The other half is that work groups – like individuals – have certain needs in common. There are three areas of overlapping need which are centrally important, as illustrated in Figure 3.1.

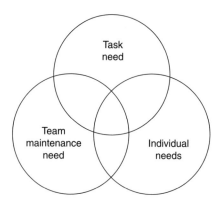

**Figure 3.1**  Overlapping needs

# TASK NEED

Work groups and organizations come into being because there is a task to be done that is too big for one person. You can climb a hill or small mountain by yourself, but you cannot climb Mount Everest on your own – you need a team for that.

Why call it a need? Because pressure builds up a head of steam to accomplish the common task. People can feel very frustrated if they are prevented from doing so.

## TEAM MAINTENANCE NEED

This is not so easy to perceive as the task need; as with an iceberg, much of the life of any group lies below the surface. The distinction that the task need concerns things and the second need involves people does not help much.

Again, it is best to think of groups that are threatened from without by forces aimed at their disintegration or from within by disruptive people or ideas. We can then see how they give priority to maintaining themselves against these external or internal pressures, sometimes showing great ingenuity in the process. Many of the written or unwritten rules of the group are designed to promote this unity and to maintain cohesiveness at all costs. Those who rock the boat or infringe group standards and corporate balance may expect reactions varying from friendly indulgence to downright anger. Instinctively a common feeling exists that 'United we stand, divided we fall', that good relationships, desirable in themselves, are also an essential means towards the shared end. This need to create and promote group cohesiveness I have called the *team maintenance* need. After all, everyone knows what a team is.

## INDIVIDUAL NEEDS

Third, individuals bring into the group their own needs – not just the physical ones for food and shelter (which are largely catered for by the payment of wages these days) but also the psychological ones: recognition; a sense of doing something worthwhile; status; and the deeper needs to give to and receive from other people in a working situation. These individual needs are perhaps more profound that we sometimes realize.

They spring from the depths of our common life as human beings. They may attract us to, or repel us from, any given group. Underlying them all is the fact that people need one another not just to survive but to achieve and develop personality.

# THE THREE CIRCLES INTERACT

Now these three areas of need overlap and influence one another. If the common task is achieved, for example, then that tends to build the team and to satisfy personal human needs in individuals. If there is a lack of cohesiveness in the team circle – a failure of team maintenance – then clearly performance in the task area will be impaired and the satisfaction of individual members reduced. Thus, as above, we can visualize the needs present in work groups as three overlapping circles.

Nowadays when I show the model on an overhead projector slide I usually colour the circles red, blue, and green, for light (not pigment) refracts into these three primary colours. It is a way of suggesting that the three circles form a universal model. In whatever field you are, at whatever level of leadership – team leader, operational leader, or strategic leader – there are three things that you should always be thinking about: *task*, *team*, and *individual*. Leadership is essentially an other-centred activity – not a self-centred one.

The three-circle model is simple but not simplistic or superficial. Keeping in mind those three primary colours, we can make an analogy with what is happening when we watch a television programme: the full-colour moving pictures are made up of dots of those three primary and (in the overlapping areas) three secondary colours. It is only when you stand well back from the complex moving and talking picture of life at work that you begin to see the underlying pattern of the three circles. Of course they are not always so balanced and clear as the model suggests, but they are nonetheless there.

# THE FUNCTIONS OF LEADERSHIP

What has all this got to do with leadership? Simply this: in order to achieve the common task and to maintain teamwork, certain *functions* have to be performed. And a function is what you *do*, as opposed to a quality, which is an aspect of what you are. For example, someone has to define the objectives, make a plan, or hold the team together if it is threatened by disruptive forces.

Now we are on firm ground. For you can learn to provide the functions of leadership which are called for by task, team and individual needs. This is the entrance door to effective leadership. The function approach set out here is also sometimes called *action-centred leadership*. A function is one of a group of related actions contributing to development or maintenance, just as each part of the body has its function in relation to the whole. It comes from a Latin word meaning *performance*. Sometimes it is used more widely to mean what I have called *role* – the special kind of activity proper to a professional position. In Figure 3.2 I have listed the main functions that are required if the task is to be achieved, the team held together, and the needs of individuals met.

It should not be supposed that a leader has to perform all these functions himself or herself. Indeed, in groups of more than five people there are too many functional contributions or activities for one person to do them all on his or her own. Functions have to be shared and sometimes – in all or part – delegated. Or, putting it another way, all team members are responsible (even if not legally-speaking accountable) for the three circles. The difference between an effective team member and an effective leader is not great; it is one more of role than of commitment to all three circles or skill in meeting the common needs.

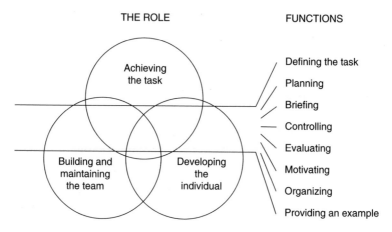

THE ROLE          FUNCTIONS

Achieving the task

Building and maintaining the team

Developing the individual

Defining the task

Planning

Briefing

Controlling

Evaluating

Motivating

Organizing

Providing an example

**Figure 3.2**  Leadership functions

Obviously decision making is potentially going to be an ingredient in all the functional domains. *Planning* is a good example. Planning means building a mental bridge from where you are now to where you want to be when you have achieved the objective before you. The function of planning meets the group's need to accomplish its task by answering the question *how*. But the 'how' question soon leads to 'When does this or that have to happen?' and 'Who does what?'

From the leadership perspective, the key issue is how far you should make the plan yourself or how far you should share the planning function with your team. Let's look at the options.

There is a lot to be said for moving as far to the right end of the continuum as you can (see Figure 3.3). For *the more people share in decisions that affect their working life the more they are motivated to carry them out.* That consideration, however, has to be balanced against the fact that the wider you open the door of the Inn of Decision the less control you have of the outcome. The team may make a plan that, although meeting the requirements you have identified, is not the way you would have done it yourself. Can you live with that?

**Use of authority by the leader**

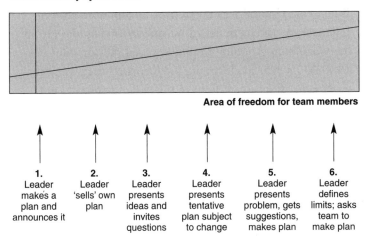

**Area of freedom for team members**

| 1.<br>Leader makes a plan and announces it | 2.<br>Leader 'sells' own plan | 3.<br>Leader presents ideas and invites questions | 4.<br>Leader presents tentative plan subject to change | 5.<br>Leader presents problem, gets suggestions, makes plan | 6.<br>Leader defines limits; asks team to make plan |

**Figure 3.3** The planning continuum

Just where you should act on the planning continuum depends on several key factors, notably *the time available to plan* and *the competence level of the team members*. There is no one right 'style'. The best leaders are consistent – you know where you stand with them and they are in many respects predictable. But when it comes to decision making they are infinitely flexible. So a good leader, working with individuals or teams, will operate at different points on the scale during a day.

Once work has started on the plan, it may be necessary to revise or adapt the plan as circumstances or conditions dictate. Again, you must steer a middle course between the perennial need for flexibility as change unfolds and a certain persistence or tenacity in sticking to the agreed plan. Certainly, allowing too many unnecessary changes in the plan can itself breed confusion. As the military proverb says, *Order – counter-order – disorder.*

Always remember that everyone who works for you has 10,000 million brain cells. If time allows, it is always worthwhile to listen to people. You will be constantly surprised at the quality of the thinking and ideas available to you.

When Fort Dunlop was taken over by Sumitomo, the Japanese management asked for money-saving ideas from the workforce. A junior employee saved the company £100,000 a year in electricity payments by suggesting that every other fluorescent light in the huge factory did not need to be used – an idea that he had had for years!

In fact you should develop a habit of listening for ideas, whether with a particular decision in mind or as a wider strategy. There are plenty of ideas around for those who are ready to receive them. That great business leader Roy Thompson capitalized some of this potential wealth:

*The way I look at it, everyone has an idea and one in a dozen may be a good idea. If you have to talk to a dozen people to get one good idea, even just the glimmering of an idea, that isn't wasteful work. People are continually passing things on to me, because I have given them to believe that I will be interested, I might even pay for it! Sometimes, usually when it is least expected, something comes up that is touched with gold.*

In summary, the degree to which you as a leader can share decisions differs according to such factors as the situation – especially the time available – and the relative and relevant knowledge of the team members. Actually deciding where to decide on a continuum that has *control* at one end and *freedom* at the other is in itself an important decision when working with others. Here are some questions to ask yourself:

# CHECKLIST

|  | Yes | No |
|---|---|---|
| Have you agreed the aims and objectives with the team? | ☐ | ☐ |
| Have you involved the team in the collecting and sifting of the relevant information? | ☐ | ☐ |
| Has the team helped you to generate a number of possible courses of action? | ☐ | ☐ |
| Have you used the synergy of the team members' minds to firm up the feasible options? | ☐ | ☐ |
| Have you tested for consensus to see how far, in the circumstances, a course of action you favour is seen to be the optimum one? | ☐ | ☐ |
| Have you secured everyone's commitment to make it work? | ☐ | ☐ |
| Have you reviewed the decision with the team so that the lessons of success and failure are learnt for the future? | ☐ | ☐ |

# KEY POINTS

- Thinking is both solitary and social. We need to think for ourselves – and make time to do so. But we also need to talk with and listen to others, for stimulus and encouragement, fresh perspectives and new ideas. Conversation at its best is a form of mutual thinking.

- The role of a leader is defined by the three circles of need – task, team and individual – and the responding set of functions. Communication and decision making are complementary dimensions. A key issue for all leaders is how far they should share decisions with their team or colleagues.

- The more you share decisions the higher the quality of the decision is likely to be. Moreover, the more that people share decisions which directly affect their working life, the more they tend to be motivated to implement them. Yet the exigency of the situation – shortage of time and the crisis factor – sometimes restricts the scope for sharing. And you also have to remember that the more you share a decision the less control you have over the resulting decision's quality and direction. So you need judgement here.

- When the decision-making process is over, you still have to take the decision.

- Outside the confines of the making of a particular decision you should always be open to the ideas, suggestions and information that people offer you. The more you show interest, the more that people will tell you. Ten per cent of their ideas are lined with gold.

> **Three cobblers with their wits combined**
> **Equal Zhage Liag, the master mind.**
> CHINESE PROVERB

# KEY PROBLEM-SOLVING STRATEGIES

Decision making, problem solving, and creative thinking have in common the fact that they are all forms of effective thinking. But there are some distinctions between them. You can, for example, think creatively, in the sense of having an original idea, without either making a decision or solving a problem. In this chapter the main focus is upon problem solving.

## HOW PROBLEMS DIFFER FROM DECISIONS

What is a problem? A 'problem' is literally 'something thrown in front of you'. Another of those Greek words by origin, it is related to 'ballistics'. Originally what was thrown or put in front of one by the Greek teachers was the sort of puzzle or question that you encountered in the first chapter: 'The nine dots', 'The six matchsticks' and 'Who owns the zebra?' (Incidentally, has your Depth Mind come up with solutions – or extra solutions – to the first two yet?)

You will notice that in problems like these, all the elements of the solution are already there. All that you have to do is arrange or rearrange what has been given. In that sense, a problem is a solution in disguise.

As a result of solving such problems your life is not going to be different. By contrast, a decision usually *does* mean that life will be different. It opens the way to changes of some kind or other. Some of these changes are planned, wanted, expected or at least foreseen (the manifest consequences), whereas others are not. But solving or not solving a crossword puzzle is not going to change your life in any way.

In this respect such problems are similar to games – in fact, games are sets of problems. Why do we invent them? Because there is nothing that humans enjoy more than solving problems. The skills of a problem solver in this limited sense, however, differ from those of a decision maker. As a problem solver you have to be clever, with analytical skills well honed on manyother problems in that particular field. By contrast, a decision-maker needs a much wider range of skills and characteristics.

Moving away from puzzles and games, the problems we encounter in real life are mostly obstacles placed in front of us. If you decide to climb Mount Everest, for example, you may find that all goes well until – a day before your final ascent – a heavy storm suddenly develops on the South Col, the ridge leading to the summit. You have a problem! Notice that you would not have that particular problem – or any problems – on Everest unless you had made a decision to climb to the summit. It is not a problem for anyone else. And it would cease to be a problem for you if you changed your mind and decided to go off and climb some other mountain in the Himalayas.

Therefore problems as obstacles or difficulties in the path ahead of us are always secondary to the results of decision making.

Decisions create problems. One way of solving them – or rather the problem state in your mind – is to alter your decision, or at least your plan. Did you have a contingency plan – a Plan B – for your route up the mountain if the weather deteriorated or avalanches (unexpected at this time of year) occurred?

If you stick with your decision, then, in consultation with your team, you have to find a way of overcoming the problem. Because the mental framework you must use is so similar to the decision-making process, a single model covering them both is possible.

# A UNIFIED MODEL FOR DECISION MAKING AND PROBLEM SOLVING

If you are trying to cross a mountain stream you will jump from rock to rock, zig-zagging your way to the far bank. Like thinking inside your head, this is an untidy but purposeful activity. But when you have to get a team across a metaphorical river you need to be able to construct a simple bridge, so that everyone knows where they are in the decision-making/problem-solving discussion. (See the illustration below.)

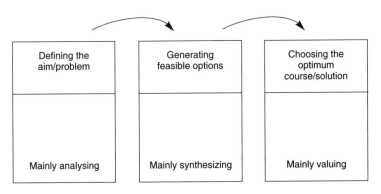

| Defining the aim/problem | Generating feasible options | Choosing the optimum course/solution |
| --- | --- | --- |
| Mainly analysing | Mainly synthesizing | Mainly valuing |

**Figure 4.1** The bridge model

You can see that the skills required, as one phase merges into the next, change. A new function with its family of more specific skills comes into play. The model is useful for your team as well as yourself. It can help everyone to keep in step.

# ASKING THE RIGHT QUESTIONS

A key skill, both when you are thinking something through by yourself and when you are leading or participating in a team, is to *ask the right questions*. Questions are the spanners that unlock the mind. Here are the kinds of questions you should ask yourself – and others.

## Understanding the problem

- When did you first sense or become aware of the problem or the need for a decision?

- Have you defined the problem or objective in your own words? (Remember that a problem properly defined is a problem half-solved.)

- Are there any other possible definitions of the problem worth considering? What general solutions do they suggest?

- Are you clear about what you are trying to do? Where are you now and where do you want to get to?

- Have you identified the important factors and salient facts? Do you need to spend more time on obtaining more information? Do you know the relevant policies, rules, limitations, and procedures?

- Have you reduced the problem to its simplest terms without oversimplifying it?

## Towards solving the problem

- Have you checked all your main assumptions?

- Out of all the possible courses or solutions, have you identified a shortlist of the feasible ones?

- Can you eliminate some of these in order to shorten the list still further?

- If no solution or course of action seems right by itself, can you synthesize elements in two or more solutions to create an effective way of dealing with the problem?

- Have you clearly identified the criteria by which the feasible options must be judged?

- If you are still stuck, can you imagine yourself in the end-state where you want to be? If so, can you work backwards from there to where you are now?

- Has anyone else faced this problem? How did they solve it?

## Evaluating the decision and implementing it

- Have you used all the available information?

- Have you checked your solution from all angles?

- Are you clear about the manifest consequences?

- Have you an implementation plan with dates or times for completion?

- Is the plan realistic?

- Do you have a contingency plan if things do not work out as expected?

- When are you and your team planning to review the decision in the light of experience?

You may feel rather overwhelmed by this long list of questions. But you do not have to ask them all every time you are involved in making decisions or solving problems, for some of the questions will already have clear answers. What you should develop are three levels of competence:

- *Awareness* of problems or the need for decisions – either actual or potential. Have your feelers out, so that you are not taken by surprise.

- *Understanding* of where you and the team are in relation to the problem or decision. In what phase of the bridge model (see page 45) are you? Does more work need to be done on analysing information and defining the problem or decision? Or are you in the business of generating feasible options?

- *Skill* in asking the right questions of the right people at the right time, and being able to test the answers for their truth content. Action based on truth is much more likely to be effective than action based on a faulty perception of reality.

It may all sound like hard work. You recall Roy Thompson's words about 'thinking until it hurts' and 'this arduous and tiring work'. Yes, yes – but it is also great fun. It is what life is all about! I repeat: there is nothing more satisfying than being faced with a mental challenge and overcoming it. The harder the problem, the more elation you and your team will feel when you overcome it. So resolve to enjoy decision making and problem solving. The more you enjoy something the more of it you will want to do – and the better at it you will get.

# HOW TO APPROACH SYSTEMS PROBLEMS

Obstacle-type problems account for 80 per cent of the problems that leaders encounter, but you should also be aware of systems

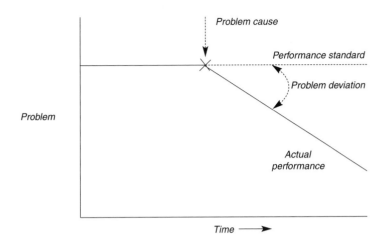

**Figure 4.2** Systems problems

problems – the other 20 per cent. If you are a technical specialist, of course, those proportions are reversed and the majority of your working time will be spent on systems problems.

A system is a whole made up of integrated parts. It can be organic (your body), mechanical (your car engine), or a process (your system for billing customers). A systems problem is essentially a deviation from the norm. We can represent it visually by two lines (see the illustration above). The greater the difference between the normal performance (how the system is supposed to work) and the active performance (what is actually happening), the bigger the problem.

The main strategy in systems problems is to find the point of deviation and then establish what caused it. The first aim is to establish the exact time and place of that critical deviation. What happened? When? How much? Who was affected? Who saw it? And so on. Notice again that the key skill of asking the right questions is in play, focusing on the deviation point on the diagram.

# EXERCISE 3  THE W5H FORMULA

Choose any systems problem facing you and practise your question skills – Who?, What?, Where?, When?, Why? and How? See if you can pinpoint the deviation from the normal working of the system in question.

Once you have done that, list the possible causes. Now begin to eliminate the causes that can be proved innocent. You will be left with two or three suspects.

Having established when and where the deviation occurred, you then have to identify the cause or causes. Only by tackling these can you really solve a systems problem. Treat causes, not symptoms, if it is possible to do so.

Plastec Ltd – a company making plastic containers – discovered that a rising percentage of its output was developing cracks. A project group studied the manufacturing process in detail and eventually defined the points of deviation: a change of supplier and a failure to clean out some storage vats. The new supplier inadvertently used these storage vats, and the plastic therefore became contaminated. Once the causes had been identified, the systems were altered to prevent any repetition, and the problem did not recur.

Beware of the fallacy of the single cause. In relatively simple problems there is only one cause but, in more complex ones, two or three causes may be combining to produce the unwanted effect. In the case study on Plastec Ltd you will have noticed that it was the combination of two changes from the norm – a new supplier and poor cleaning procedures – that produced the problem.

# KEY POINTS

- Problems come in two main forms: problems that are really obstacles that appear across your chosen path, and systems problems.

- The broad approach to both families of problems and to decision making is the same. It can be compared to building a bridge across a river on three pillars:

  *Defining the problem*

  *Generating feasible options*

  *Choosing the optimum course/solution*

- A key thinking skill for an effective problem-solver is asking the right questions – to oneself initially but also to others. Questions are the spanners that unlock the problem in the mind, or at least the gates that bar entry to it. 'To act is easy,' said Goethe, 'to think is hard.'

- Systems problems are best approached by regarding them as deviations from an expected norm. Diagnosis includes identifying and establishing the exact nature of that deviation and what caused it. The solution – if one is possible – is to remove the cause of the problem. A secondary strategy for a problem solver where 'cure' isn't possible is to mitigate the effects of the problem on the performance of the system as a whole.

- People who are good with hammers see every problem as a nail.

> **One should never impose one's views on a problem; one should rather study it, and in time a solution will reveal itself.**
> ALBERT EINSTEIN

# HOW TO GENERATE IDEAS

**To raise new questions, new possibilities, to regard old problems from a new angle, requires creative imagination.**
ALBERT EINSTEIN

When you are stuck in problem solving – that is, when the techniques you have applied successfully in the past are not working – try a more creative thinking approach. You may be trying to dig the same hole deeper, worrying at your problem like a terrier, when perhaps you should be digging your hole somewhere else.

## BRAINSTORMING

The best-known and most widely used creative thinking technique is brainstorming. It was introduced in the 1930s, so it has been around a long time – a sign of its usefulness. You can employ its principles when you are thinking alone, but they work better in a team setting.

When brainstorming, don't overlook the obvious! The obvious solution is sometimes the best. It may not, anyway, be obvious to everyone; and it may be possible to twist an obvious idea into something not so obvious. Don't fear repetition, either! Accusing someone of being repetitive is a form of adverse criticism and should be avoided. The same idea may trigger a different response at a different time in the brainstorming session.

Take the common paper clip as an example. In five minutes one brainstormer came up with the following new uses.

| | |
|---|---|
| Pipe cleaner | Fuse wire |
| Nail cleaner | Letter opener |
| Tie-clip | Catapult missile |
| Ear de-waxer | Toothpick |
| Picture hook | Cufflink |
| Small-hole poker | Ornament |
| Screwdriver | Typewriter cleaner |
| Fishing hook | Tension reducer (like worry beads) |
| Broken bra-strap mender | Zip-fastener tag mender |

I expect you can do even better than that! Are you ready to have a go? Look at the Guidelines opposite first.

## EXERCISE 4   BRAINSTORMING SKILLS

Take a pair of scissors and list 50 new uses for them – apart from cutting things.

You have 10 minutes. Write your ideas down and – if stuck – go back and build on your first 10 ideas.

# GUIDELINES FOR BRAINSTORMING

**Suspend judgement**

Give imagination the green light by withholding the critical evaluation of ideas until later. Accept ideas without judging them.

**Welcome free-wheeling**

Take off the brakes in your mind and go with the flow of your ideas. The more unusual the idea, the better – it is easier to tone down than think up.

**Strive for quantity**

The greater the number of oysters, the more likely you are to find some pearls in them.

**Combine and improve**

Listen to the ideas of others and see if you can build on them. Their way-out ideas may stimulate some buried memories or sleeping brain cells in your Depth Mind.

**Do not edit**

Ideas should not be elaborated or defended, just quickly stated and recorded.

One major reason why brainstorming is useful is that it helps to free us from 'functional fixedness'. We have a fixed idea, for example, that a thing has only one function and that is what it is there for. By banning the use of that familiar function (in the case of scissors, the function of cutting), the mind is released to consider other possibilities. With a little adaptation, scissors would make an interesting geometrical instrument.

Take the modern British Army bayonet. Did you know that it is ingeniously designed to combine with its scabbard to form a pair of wirecutters? Or that it has a third function (officially!) built into it – that of a bottle-opener?

*Pilkington Brothers Limited in the UK had a technical problem...* During the final inspection of sheet glass, small globules of water were identified by the inspection machine as flaws in the glass. A brainstorming session produced 29 ideas in less than five minutes. After research and development, three of these were used in the system, which solved the problem.

*H J Heinz in the USA had a marketing problem...* The company wanted to get sales promotional material to consumers more quickly. Brainstorming produced 195 ideas. After evaluation, eight were immediately used. A member of Heinz, when talking about another brainstorming session, said, 'Brainstorming generated more and better ideas than our special committee produced in 10 meetings.'

The essential principle behind brainstorming is simple. Please refer back to Chapter 1 and the three functions of analysing, synthesizing and valuing. What brainstorming commands you to do is to make a temporary and conscious division between synthesizing on the one hand and valuing on the other – for much of our valuing is negative and premature, like unseasonable frost that kills off the buds of spring. As Jean-Paul Sartre once said, 'Criticism often takes from the tree caterpillars and blossoms together.' Brainstorming's suspension of judgement is an invitation to exercise some inner mental discipline. Analysing and valuing have their time and place, but your imagination has wings – let it fly free!

# HOW TO RUN A BRAINSTORMING SESSION

No more than 10 people should be involved. Some may know about the field, others may not – a mixture of both is desirable. They should ideally have been trained in the brainstorming technique before the meeting. When you run the session:

- Define the problem (using your analytical and briefing skills).

- Help people to understand the problem by highlighting the background information and history.

- Clarify the aim in a succinct sentence: 'In how many ways can we...?'

- Have a brief warm-up session, using a common problem or object.

- Brainstorm 70 ideas in 20 minutes, or a similar target. One person should write up the ideas on a flipchart. Allow time for silent reflection. Check that no critical remarks are made. Encourage cross-fertilization.

- Establish criteria for selecting the feasible ideas. Choose the best.

- Reverse brainstorm: 'In how many ways can this idea fail?'

About 40 minutes is the optimum time for a brainstorming session. But you should ask the participants to go on considering the problem and let you have further suggestions. Remember that they have programmed their Depth Minds by the brainstorming session, and other ideas will come to them unexpectedly.

A leading US firm of jigsaw-puzzle makers held a brainstorming session to think up ideas for new puzzles. It produced some worthy ideas but nothing brilliant. A month later, one of the participants went to see an exhibition of Tutankhamun's treasures in Washington DC. The gold mask of the pharaoh struck him as a great jigsaw puzzle idea! He was right – it broke all records for jigsaw puzzle sales in the United States.

# KEY POINTS

- Being creative involves the use of the imagination or original ideas in order to create something. Creative thinking is that part of it which produces the new ideas.

- 'It is the function of creative people', writes the poet William Ploner, 'to perceive the relations between thoughts, or things, or forms of expression that may seem utterly different, and to be able to combine them into some new forms – *the power to connect the seemingly unconnected*.'

- Brainstorming is a useful technique, for generating ideas, whether you practise it on your own or in a team context. The essence of it is to make a temporary wall in the mind between the analysing/synthesizing functions on the one side, and the (critical) valuing function on the other side.

- Ideas rarely arrive in this world fully-formed and gift-wrapped. With a little practice you can learn to *build on ideas*, to take the germs of success in someone else's half-baked idea and to develop it towards fruition. By the same warrant, allow others to build on your ideas for the common good. Only God owns the intellectual property rights to truth.

- 'I start where the last man left off', said the inventor Thomas Edison.

- Creativity is so delicate a flower that praise tends to make it bloom, while discouragement often nips it in the bud. *Any of us will put out more and better ideas if our efforts are appreciated.*

> **Creative thinking thrives in an environment of mutual stimulation, feedback and constructive criticism –**
> **in a community of creativity.**
> ANON

# THINKING OUTSIDE THE BOX

Valuable though brainstorming is, not least as an introduction to one or two of the fundamental principles of creative thinking, it is not the whole story. To develop your skills as a creative problem-solver you need to adopt and practise the strategies set out below.

## TOWARDS A MORE CREATIVE APPROACH

Brainstorming challenges one kind of unconscious assumption, namely that hammers are for knocking in nails or that scissors are for cutting. But there are other forms of unconscious assumption that may inhibit your thinking.

Take the 'Nine dots' and 'Six matchsticks' problems in Chapter 1. The reason why many people cannot do the first one is that they put an unconscious or invisible framework around the dots, and try to solve the problem within it. That is impossible. But if you break out of that self-imposed limitation, the solution to the problem is easily reached. (See 'The nine dots' solution below.)

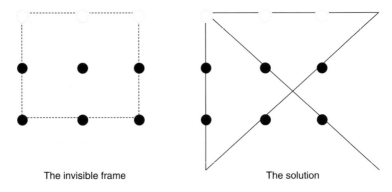

The invisible frame          The solution

**Figure 6.1** 'The nine dots' solution

Incidentally, I first published 'The nine dots' problem in 1969, in a book called *Training for Decisions*. It was the origin of a new phrase in the English language, now credited to me – *thinking outside the box*.

There is a similar assumption made in the second problem. People *assume* that they must arrange the six matches in a pattern of four equilateral triangles in only one plane. If they take one small step and give themselves permission to place the matches on top of one another, they can reach the first solution. But if they break out of the two-dimensional constraint into three dimensions, they achieve the most elegant solution.

Please don't mistake me: you cannot think without *making assumptions*. But they should be conscious ones from which you can retreat when they become indefensible. The assumptions that trip you up are the unconscious ones, the constraints or limitations that you are not aware of. That is one reason why effective thinking needs social interaction. We need critical input from others to remove these filters from our eyes.

A senior manager in the UK marketing department of Hoover, the household appliance company, once had the bright idea of introducing a 'free flights' promotional scheme as an incentive for buying their products. It was a spectacularly bad decision. Some 200,000 people flew with the scheme, but it cost the company

Star of David                          Pyramid

**Figure 6.2**  'The six matchsticks' solution

around £48 million. Some 127 people sought compensation in the courts, facing Hoover with a possible bill of millions of pounds if they succeeded. The president of Hoover Europe was dismissed from his £500,000-a-year post, and the US owners quickly sold the company for a knock-down price. You do not get decision making more wrong than that.

Why did this fiasco happen? Because the Hoover managers concerned made a *false assumption*. They assumed that when most of the people who bought appliances saw the small print wrapped about the 'free flights' offer – the complex restrictions and qualifications they deliberately built in to deter applicants – these new customers would not bother to go through such a complex approach for the sake of a free air ticket. They underestimated the public! Enough people persevered in finding a route through all the complex rules and conditions that their free flights brought the company to its knees.

This true story is a parable to remind us of the importance of checking to ensure that we are not allowing unconscious assumptions to act like hidden reefs and rip the bottom of the ship.

# LOOK WIDER FOR SOLUTIONS

My phrase *thinking outside the box* ties in with the concept of lateral thinking, introduced by the well-known thinker and writer Edward de Bono in *The Five Day Course in Thinking* (1968).

Lateral thinking means abandoning the step-by-step approach and thinking, as it were, 'to one side'.

| Vertical thinking | Lateral thinking |
|---|---|
| Chooses | Changes |
| Looks for what is right | Looks for what is different |
| One thing must follow | Makes deliberate jumps directly from another |
| Concentrates on relevance | Welcomes chance intrusions |
| Moves in the most likely directions | Explores the least likely directions |

The sideways (or lateral) thinking involved often leads to reversing what appears to be the natural or logical way of doing things. For example, the earliest method of making cars involved teams of men moving from one car to another. Henry Ford turned it all upside down. He put the car frames on belts and moved them past the men – the birth of the assembly line.

It is important to think sideways because the seeds of a solution to a problem may lie outside the box you are working in. Really creative people have a wide span of relevance: they look far afield, even to remote places or times in history, for solutions to the problems they face. When the eighteenth-century agriculturalist Jethro Tull invented the seed drill he summoned up his previous experience as an organist: he was creatively transferring technology from one area to another. Most of us, however, tend to think in compartments, and the divisions in work that make specialization possible encourage this blinkered thinking.

Always be willing to challenge widely accepted assumptions.

As the exercise 'The nine dots' and 'The six matches' illustrate, thinking outside the box means being able to spot assumptions, habits or customary ways of thinking that are widely and uncritically accepted but have no basis in reality. Many of these we breathe in by virtue of the society in which we live. They are among the everyday conventions we accept as truths without too much examination. 'As everybody knows...'

---

### When 'everyone knows' something to be true, nobody knows nothing

Andy Grove, later the Chairman of Intel, always remembered the oft-repeated saying of one of his professors when he was a student: 'When everybody knows that something is so, it means that nobody knows nothing.' It stayed with him throughout his career, and he gave the following example of its relevance.

'Our little research group at Fairchild [Semi-conductor] some 40 years ago started to study the characteristics of surface layers that were the heart of modern integrated circuits. At that time, "everybody knew" that surface states, an artifice of quantum mechanics, would interfere with us building such chips. As it turns out, nobody knew nothin': We never found any surface states; what we found was trace contamination. When we identified and removed this, the road opened up to the chip industry as we know it today.'

---

# HOW TO USE YOUR DEPTH MIND

Creative thinking cannot be forced. If you are working on a problem and getting nowhere, it is often best to leave it for a while and let your subconscious – your Depth Mind – take over. Your mind does not work by the clock, although it likes deadlines. Sometimes the answer will come to you in the middle of the night.

Grasping the principle of the Depth Mind could open the way for you to a more creative approach to problem solving. Many people are still not even aware that their depth minds can carry out important mental functions for them, such as synthesizing parts into new wholes or establishing new connections while they are engaged in other activities.

Imagine your mind to be like a personal fax machine. It would be nice and tidy if you could sit down for an hour each morning before breakfast and receive inspired fax messages from your Depth Mind. But it is not like that. The fax machine might start whirring at any time of the day or night.

If you are thinking along a certain line and nothing happens, stop. Instead of investing more time – throwing good money after bad – analyse the problem again and see if you can come up with a new approach. Usually your frustration will be caused by one of the mental roadblocks described in the table on pages 68–69.

The processes of analysing a problem or identifying an objective are themselves means of programming the mind. Possible solutions and courses of action almost instantly begin to occur to us. Where there is a time-delay this means that the deeper parts of the brain have been summoned into action and have made what contribution they can.

How important *preparation time* is for creative thinking! Careful and clear analysis, conscious imagining or synthesizing (using such techniques as brainstorming either in groups or solo), and exercising the valuing function of thought in a positive rather than negative way – all these are vital to lay the foundations for thinking creatively. (See page 67.)

If you are planning to experiment and try a session before breakfast, it is useful always to have a preparation phase the night before. Imagine yourself as a house decorator, scraping down the woodwork and filling in holes and priming here and there, prior to painting a first coat the following day.

# THE CREATIVE THINKING PROCESS

| Preparation | The hard work. You have to collect and sort the relevant information, analyse the problem as thoroughly as you can, and explore possible solutions. |
|---|---|
| Incubation | This is the Depth Mind phase. Mental work – analysing, synthesizing and valuing – continues on the problem in your subconscious mind. The parts of the problem separate and new combinations occur. These may involve other ingredients stored away in your memory. |
| Insight | The 'Eureka' moment. A new idea emerges into your conscious mind, either gradually or suddenly, like a fish flashing out of the water. These moments often occur when you are not thinking about the problem but are in a relaxed frame of mind. |
| Validation | This is where your valuing faculty comes into play. A new idea, insight, intuition, hunch or solution needs to be thoroughly tested. This is especially so if it is to form the basis for action of any kind. |

Although it is useful for you to have this framework in mind, remember that the actual mental process is a lot more untidy than the above table suggests. Think of the phases as being four notes on a piano which can be played in different sequences or combined together in complex chords.

## Mozart

'When I am completely myself,' Mozart wrote to a friend in a letter, 'entirely alone or during the night when I cannot sleep, it is on such occasions that my ideas flow best. Whence and how they come I know not nor can I force them. Nor do I hear in my imagination the parts successively, but I hear them at the same time all together.'

# MENTAL ROADBLOCKS

| | |
|---|---|
| Lack of facts | If you are not sure you have all the relevant facts, you naturally hesitate to commit yourself. Do some more research, and that may get you moving again. |
| Lack of conviction | Maybe you find it difficult because you lack conviction in the value of this exercise or the way in which you have been asked to do it. Re-establish a worthwhile objective. |
| Lack of a starting point | Possibly the problem seems so large that you do not know where to start. If so, make a start anywhere. You can always change it later. Inspiration comes after you have started, not before. |
| Lack of perspective | Perhaps you are too close to the problem, especially if you have lived with it a long time or have been worrying about it incessantly. Try leaving it for a week. Consult others. Simply explaining it to them may help. They may see new angles. |

| Lack of motivation | Do you want it to happen enough? Creative thinking requires perseverance in the face of surmountable difficulty. If you are too easily put off, it may be a sign that, deep down, you lack the necessary motivation. Reinvigorate your sense of purpose. |

The function of creative thinking in problem solving is to come up with new ideas. But remember that at some stage your valuing skills have to be brought into play. Here are six questions to ask about any new idea, solution, or course of action:

- Is it really new?

- Is it both relevant and practical?

- Whom will it involve?

- How much will it cost?

- How much will it save?

- Will it require more formal evaluation?

In times of rapid change, like our own age, there is a premium on your skills as a creative thinker. If you can think productively and constructively, as well as analytically and logically, it will give you a third dimension in all your decision making and problem solving.

# KEY POINTS

- One of the most valuable principles for improving your creative approach to work and life is to learn to *think outside the box*. Essentially that means be willing to challenge the assumptions – often unconscious – that put an invisible cage around the bird of thought.

- One form of thinking outside the box is to think sideways – lateral thinking. For sometimes the solution to a problem – at least in embryo – lies in a field of enterprise adjacent to one's own but quite distinct from it.

- There is a danger in formalizing any aspect of the creative process – it is a delicate balance between following a conscious process or framework and being guided by the mind's natural inclinations. But it is worth bearing in mind the commonsense sequence:

PREPARATION

INCUBATION

INSIGHT

VALIDATION

- INCUBATION – sitting on eggs until the young birds of ideas emerge – is a metaphor for the Depth Mind's work. We all have a purposive and helpful Depth Mind; we differ as to the use we make of it.

- 'In the creative state', writes the novelist E M Forster, 'a person is taken out of himself. He lets down as it were a bucket into his subconscious, and draws up something which is normally beyond his reach. He mixes this thing with his normal experience and out of the mixture something new emerges.'

> The intellect has little to do on the road to discovery. There comes a leap in consciousness, call it intuition or what you will, and the solution comes to you and you don't know how or why.
>
> ALBERT EINSTEIN

# DEVELOPING YOUR THINKING SKILLS

Winston Churchill once said, 'I am always willing to learn, but I do not like being taught.' Actually, when you learn, you are being taught – by yourself. No doubt Socrates, if he was here, could teach you how to think, but he is not here. Nor is decision making and creative problem solving a school and university subject; there is no formal body of knowledge, supported by empirical research. And so, if you truly want to develop your thinking skills, your task is essentially one of self-development. In this chapter we shall look at some common-sense guidelines that you will need if you choose to go down that road.

## WHAT IS AN EFFECTIVE PRACTICAL THINKER?

Forming a clear picture of the kind of thinker you would like to be is the first step you need to take. A clear concept of what you might be one day can act as your magnet. Remember that point about formulating where you want to be and then working backwards?

You could do it in abstract terms, listing all the qualities, the knowledge, and the functions or skills you would like to acquire by such-and-such a date. I have to admit, though, that that does not work for me: it is a bit too academic. I suggest a more homely method, which any South Sea cannibal of olden times would have relished.

In Exercise 5 below I invite you to recall people whose thinking skills you have admired. They can be people you have known personally or have studied in some depth (by, say, reading more than one biography of them). In the right-hand column, write down as concisely and specifically as you can those thinking skills that impressed you and that you would like now to 'eat' by gobbling up and inwardly digesting, so that they become part of you. Write down, for instance, any key remarks or sayings by which the person concerned encapsulated his or her practical wisdom.

## EXERCISE 5
## YOUR PERSONAL THINKING SKILL MENTORS

Name                    Thinking skill

Take some time over this exercise, and try to get a good spread across the functions (analysing, synthesizing and valuing) and the applied forms of effective thinking (decision making, problem solving and creative thinking). After all, you don't want to eat a meal composed of just one ingredient.

You will probably find it easy to come up with the names of two or three people – a parent, a friend, a life partner or a boss you have worked for – who have exemplified a thinking skill that you covet. If it is not so easy, however, to come up with many names to complete Exercise 5, leave it for a week or two. Your Depth Mind will suggest other names and other lessons – influences that may have become more subconscious.

From your list of 'appetizing' thinking skills you can begin to create a composite and imaginary picture of the perfect practical thinker. He or she would have A's analytical skills, B's rich and creative imagination, C's ability to be flexible and improvise, D's extraordinary judgement in situations of uncertainty and unpredictability, E's courage to take calculated risks, F's intuitive sense of what is really going on behind the scenes, G's lack of arrogance and openness to criticism, H's decisiveness when a decision is called for, and I's tolerance of ambiguity when the time is not ripe for a decision.

Now a perfect person with all these skills – a Mr or Ms ABCDEFGHI – does not, and never will, exist. You may know the story of the young man who searched the world for the perfect wife. After some years he found her – but, alas, she was looking for the perfect husband! Perfection will always elude you – but excellence is a possibility.

What the exercise achieves, however, is to give you an ideal to aim for. Advanced thinkers in any field tend to be lopsided: like athletes, they develop one set of muscles rather than others. Did you know that sprinters are hopeless at long-distance running? I am not advocating that you should be a perfectly balanced thinker, a kind of intellectual 'man for all seasons'. Rather, I suggest you look carefully at your field and where you see yourself positioned in it in (a) five years' time and (b) ten years' time. The ideal that you formulate should be related to your field, although, of course, not all your personal thinking skill mentors will be from that field – at least I hope not, otherwise I should suggest that your 'span of relevance' needs widening.

## CHECK THAT YOU ARE IN THE RIGHT FIELD

Thinking skills are partly generic or transferable, and partly situational. Decision making and problem solving are not abstracts: they are earthed in a particular field, with its knowledge, traditions, legends, and values.

Dimitri Comino, the founder of Dexion plc, once discussed with me a book I was writing on motivation. 'In my experience,' he said, 'it is very difficult to motivate people. It is much better to select people who are motivated already.' The same principle holds good, I believe, for thinking skills. It is actually quite difficult to teach yourself skills that are not natural to you. So choose a field that suits your natural profile as a thinker. What is the right field of work for you? (See the table below.)

## KEY FACTORS IN CHOOSING YOUR FIELD OF WORK

| What are your interests? | An interest is a state of feeling to which you wish to pay particular attention. Long-standing interests – those you naturally like – make it much easier to acquire knowledge and skills. |
|---|---|
| What are your aptitudes? | Aptitudes are your natural abilities, what you are fitted for by disposition. In particular, an aptitude is a capacity to learn or acquire a particular skill. Your aptitude may range from |

| | being a gift or talent to simply being above average. |
|---|---|
| What are the relevant factors in your temperament? | Temperament is an important factor. Some people, for example, are uncomfortable in decision-making situations of stress and danger, while others thrive on them. Some prefer to be problem solvers rather than decision makers. |

It is usually easier to identify the fields that you are not suitable for, because you lack the necessary level of interests, mental aptitude, or temperamental characteristics to do really well in them.

Let me now make the assumption that you are in the right field. You have more or less the right profile of aptitudes. You have been able, in other words, to acquire the knowledge and professional/technical skills needed and have enjoyed doing so. You have already laid the foundations of success at the team, operational and strategic levels of leadership. You will have credibility among your colleagues. Now what you have to do is focus upon the process skills – the more generic or transferable ones – in decision making and problem solving. How do you acquire them?

## HOW TO DESIGN YOUR OWN LEARNING STRATEGY

Before planning your own self-learning programme it is useful to remind yourself of the core process of learning. (See Figure 7.1)

Recall what was said above about thinking skills being partly generic and partly situational. It is when sparks jump between these two poles that learning occurs. So you need both.

Because decision making and problem solving are such central activities in any person's life we have plenty of experience of

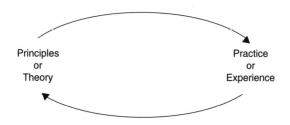

**Figure 7.1** How we learn

them. And as you move into a professional field, and begin making decisions and tackling problems, you soon build up a repertoire of experience. You learn by mistakes. In the technical aspects of your work you do have a body of knowledge – principles or theory – to bring to bear on your practice. How can you apply the same learning method to thinking skills? Here are some practical suggestions:

- Read this book again and underline all the key principles. Put a star by the models or frameworks that you can use. Build up your own body of theory.

- Make an inventory of your thinking skills in relation to your own field of work. What is the present profile of your strengths, and what are the areas for improvement?

- See if you can identify three outstanding decision makers and problem solvers in your field to whom you have access. Ask if you may interview them briefly to discover what principles – if any – have informed their own development as applied thinkers.

- Select one really bad decision made by your organization during the last 18 months. Write it up as a case study, limiting yourself to five key lessons to be learned about decision making. If you want to develop your moral courage, send it to the chief executive!

- Now select any outstanding innovation in your field, inside your organization or outside it. By an 'innovation' I mean a new idea that has been successfully 'brought to market' as a new (or renewed) product or service. Again, write it up as a case study and highlight at the end the five or six key lessons for creative problem-solvers.

- Set yourself a book-reading programme. 'He would say that, wouldn't he?' But I do not have to persuade you to read books – you have just read this one. If you have enjoyed it, and found it worthwhile, try to read one general book each year on leadership (see Further Reading for some suggestions) and one biography of an outstanding person in your field. Again, underline the key principles in pencil. Surely you can budget time for one book in 52 weeks?

- Transfer your growing body of principles, examples, practical tips, sayings or quotations, and thumbnail case studies to a stiff-covered notebook. As it fills up, take it on the occasional train journey or flight and read it reflectively, relating it to your current experience.

- Take any opportunities that come your way to attend courses or seminars that offer you know-how in the general area of effective thinking. You should, for example, become thoroughly versed in what information technology can do – and not do – at present in your field, and become skilled in the use of computers.

- Lastly, go out of your way to seek criticism of yourself as a decision maker and problem solver. However savage, however apparently negative the criticism, you still need it in order to learn. It is the toughest part of being a self-learner, but remember the sporting adage, 'No pain, no gain.' Your critics, whatever their motives or manners, are doing you the service of true friends. Sift through their comments for the gold-dust of truth.

In any self-learning programme, experience is going to play the major part. There is no getting away from that. But if you rely *just* on learning in what has been called 'the university of experience' you will be too old when you graduate to benefit much from the course! And the fees you will pay on the way will be extremely high. Short though it is, this book gives you those essential components – the key frameworks and principles – that you can use to cut down the time you take to learn by experience – experience and principles.

You will begin to develop both your knowledge of these process skills and your ability to apply that knowledge in all the challenging and potentially rewarding situations that lie ahead of you. Good luck!

# KEY POINTS

- Knowledge is only a rumour until it is in the muscle, says a Papua New Guinea proverb. Think of your mind as a muscle – or a set of muscles. This book tells you in an introductory way how to develop those muscles, but it is you who have to put in the effort. Are you keen to do so?

- Don't think of *thinking* as being hard, painful or laborious – if you do that you certainly won't apply yourself to shaping and sharpening your thinking skills. Thinking is fun, even when – or especially when – we are faced with apparently insurmountable difficulties.

- You are more likely to be effective as a practical thinker if you succeed in finding your vocation, your right niche in the world of work. The guide here is to choose a function and field of work that is optimum for your *interests*, *aptitudes* and *temperament*.

- 'I have never met a man so ignorant', said Galileo, 'that I couldn't learn something from him.' Prize especially those people you meet – in person or in books – who can teach you things in how to think.

- Practical wisdom should be your aim as a thinker, especially in the applied domain of decision making. Practical wisdom is a mixture of intelligence, experience and goodness.

    **I learn most, not from those who taught me but from those who talked with me.**
    ST AUGUSTINE

# APPENDIX SOLUTION TO 'WHO OWNS THE ZEBRA?'

This problem can be solved by analytical and logical thinking – deductive logic – and persistence! It is necessary to compile a matrix.

Roughly half-way through the problem-solving process there are two forks in the road, or mental leaps. The only way to find out which way to go is by trial and error. If you choose the wrong road, you have to retrace your steps. You can see now why the world record for finding the solution is 10 minutes!

The following is one way of solving the problem.

Keep working through the facts from 1 to 15 in sequence.

Concentrate on clues for which there is only one answer. That is:

1 There are five houses, each with a front door of a different colour, and inhabited by people of different nationalities, with different pets and drinks. Each person eats a different kind of food.

9 Milk is drunk in the middle house.

10 The Norwegian lives in the first house on the left.

15 The Norwegian lives next to the house with the blue door.

Then look for information that has only two possible answers. This is the first mental leap. That is:

6 The house with the green door is immediately to the right (your right) of the house with the ivory door.

If you place the ivory door in the middle, with the green door on its right, the answer is wrong, but you can still progress to find out who drinks the water. However, you can go no further.

If you place the ivory door in the fourth house, with the green door on the far right, this answer is correct and you can progress logically, since you will find that other items of information now have only one answer. That is:

2 The Australian lives in the house with the red door.

4 Coffee is drunk in the house with the green door.

8 Apples are eaten in the house with the yellow door.

12 Apples are eaten in the house next to the house where the horse is kept.

Then look for information that has only two possible answers. This is the second mental leap. That is:

3 The Italian owns the dog.

If you place the Italian in the house with the green door you are wrong, but you can still find out who drinks the water.

If you place the Italian in the house with the ivory door you are correct and you can progress logically, since you find other items of information now have only one answer. That is:

5 The Ukrainian drinks tea.

13 The cake-eater drinks orange juice.

Therefore the Norwegian drinks water.

14 The Japanese eats bananas.

7 The mushroom-eater owns snails.

11 The person who eats onions lives in the house next to the person with the fox.

Therefore the Japanese owns the zebra.

Another way of solving this problem is to form a matrix using nationalities rather than house numbers:

| Front doors | yellow | blue | red | ivory | green |
|---|---|---|---|---|---|
| Inhabitants | *Norwegian* | Ukrainian | Australian | Italian | *Japanese* |
| Pets | fox | horse | snails | dog | *zebra* |
| Drinks | *water* | tea | milk | orange juice | coffee |
| Food | apples | onions | mushrooms | cake | bananas |

# FURTHER READING

Alder, H (1995) *Think Like a Leader: 150 top business leaders show you how their minds work*, Piatkus, London

de Bono, E (1968) *The Five Day Course in Thinking*, McGraw-Hill, Maidenhead

de Bono, E (1971) *Lateral Thinking for Management*, McGraw-Hill, Maidenhead

de Bono, E (1971) *The Use of Lateral Thinking*, Penguin, London

de Bono, E (1985) *Six Thinking Hats*, Penguin, London

Buzan, T (1974) *Use Your Head*, BBC Publications, London

Culligan, M J, Deakins, C S and Young, A H (1983) *Back to Basics Management*, Facts on File, New York

Dawson, R (1994) *Make the Right Decision Every Time*, Nicholas Brealey, London

Drucker, P (1966) *The Effective Executive*, Harper & Row, New York

Drucker, P (1967) *The Practice of Management*, Heinemann, London

Kepner, C H and Tregoe, B (1965) *The Rational Manager*, McGraw-Hill, London

Koestler, A (1964) *The Act of Creation*, Hutchinson, London

Rawlinson, J G (1983) *Creative Thinking and Brainstorming*, Gower, Aldershot

Thompson, R (1975) *After I Was Sixty*, Hamish Hamilton, London

# By the same author

*Effective Decision Making* (1985), Pan, London
*Effective Innovation* (1996), Pan, London
*Effective Leadership Masterclass* (1996), Pan, London
*How to Grow Leaders* (2005), Kogan Page, London
*The Inspirational Leader* (2005), Kogan Page, London
*Leadership and Motivation* (2006), Kogan Page, London
*Not Bosses But Leaders* (2006), Kogan Page, London

# INDEX

Note: Page numbers in **bold** type denote **figures**

# Creating Success series

*Dealing with Difficult People* by Roy Lilley
*Decision Making & Problem Solving* by John Adair
*Develop Your Assertiveness* by Sue Bishop
*Develop Your Leadership Skills* by John Adair
*Develop Your Presentation Skills* by Theo Theobald
*Effective NLP Skills* by Richard Youell and Christina Youell
*How to Deal with Stress* by Stephen Palmer and Cary Cooper
*How to Manage People* by Michael Armstrong
*How to Organize Yourself* by John Caunt
*How to Write a Business Plan* by Brian Finch
*How to Write a Marketing Plan* by John Westwood
*How to Write Reports & Proposals* by Patrick Forsyth
*Improve Your Communication Skills* by Alan Barker
*Successful Project Management* by Trevor Young
*Successful Time Management* by Patrick Forsyth
*Taking Minutes of Meetings* by Joanna Gutmann

The above titles are available from all good bookshops.
For further information on these and other Kogan Page titles,
  or to order online, visit the Kogan Page website at
  www.koganpage.com